D1826659

This belongs to:

_____

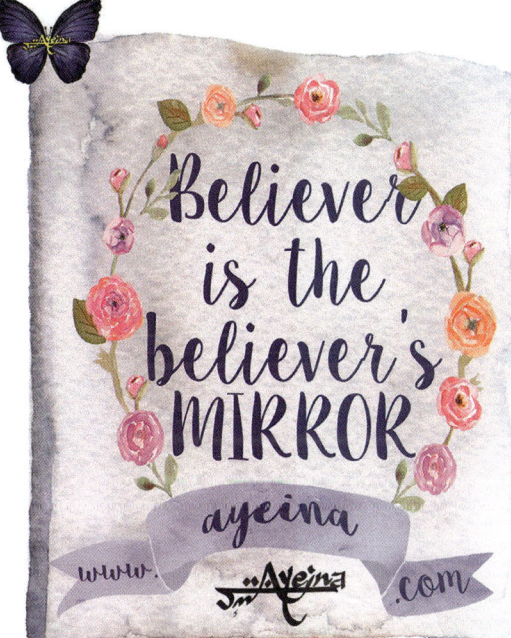

الْمُؤْمِنُ مِرْآةُ الْمُؤْمِنِ

Believer is the believer's MIRROR

ayeina

www. Ayeina .com

For permission requests,
write to
editor@ayeina.com

Mirror is to reflections.
Reflections is to thoughts.
Every life is a story,
every story is beautiful.

AYEINA IS A HUB FOR ISLAMIC REFLECTIONS/LIFESTYLE, PARENTING, EDUCATION, ART AND HUMOR.

Ayeina's Instagram account (@ayeina_official) is dedicated to #AlhamdulillahForSeries which aims to spread joy & gratitude towards Allah, in places we sometimes forget to see.

لَئِن شَكَرْتُمْ لَأَزِيدَنَّكُمْ

If you are grateful,

I will surely increase you

(Quran 14:7)

#AlhamdulillahFor

BasicNecessities

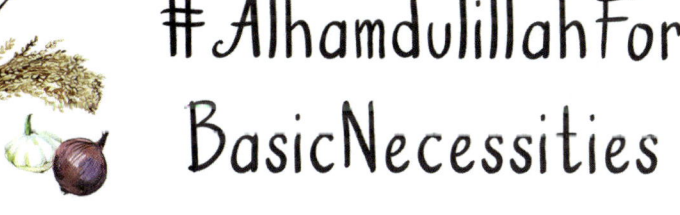

For the first week of gratitude, think about basic necessities in your life.
The illustrations for each day will simply help you think over the given weekly theme.
Start your day focusing on things you simply can't live without.
Then before you go to sleep or at any time of the day, write one thing that you'd like to say "Alhamdulillah" for.
Do this each day for a whole week until you finish all the 7 given spaces from day 1 to day 7.

Alhamdulillah for

warm clothes in winter

Alhamdulillah for

roof over our heads

Alhamdulillah for

sleep as an ultimate body recharger

Alhamdulillah for

Home cooked meal

Alhamdulillah for

access to education

Alhamdulillah for

fruits and vegetables to strengthen our body

Alhamdulillah for

halal meat anywhere anytime

WEEK 1: Write your weekly Alhamdulillah list

Day #	Alhamdulillah for . . .
1:	
2:	
3:	
4:	
5:	
6:	
7:	

NOTES

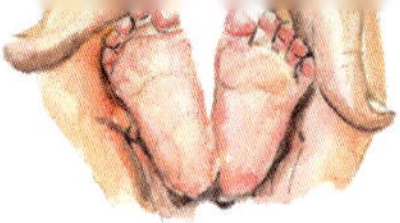

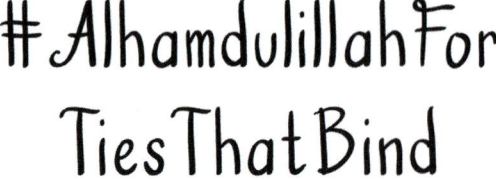

#AlhamdulillahFor

TiesThatBind

For the second week
of gratitude,
think about relationships
in your life.
The ties that bind your soul
to each other.
It could be your blood relations,
your pet, your teacher
or even a helpful stranger.
Who are you grateful for and why?
Do this each day for a whole week
until you finish all the 7 given spaces
from day 8 to day 14.

Alhamdulillah for

Family's support in rainy days

Alhamdulillah for

friends who pray with us

Alhamdulillah for

furry little pets

Alhamdulillah for

Parents who taught me right from wrong

Alhamdulillah for

friends in deen who are friends indeed

Alhamdulillah for

people who make dua for us

Alhamdulillah for

a perfect example to follow

Day #	Alhamdulillah for . . .
8 :	
9 :	
10 :	
11 :	
12 :	
13 :	
14 :	

NOTES

#AlhamdulillahFor Islam

For the third week
of gratitude,
think about spiritual growth
in your life.
Why are you Muslim?
What do you love about Islam?
What are you grateful for,
when it comes to your spirituality?
Do this each day for a whole week
until you finish all the 7 given spaces
from day 15 to day 21.

Alhamdulillah for

an imaan-boosting spiritual journey

Alhamdulillah for

a heart that only fears Allah

Alhamdulillah for

Qur'an in Arabic

Alhamdulillah for

faith as strong as a palm tree

Alhamdulillah for

blessings in halal income

Alhamdulillah for

a mosque nearby

Alhamdulillah for

reward of planting a tree

Day #	Alhamdulillah for . . .
15 :	
16 :	
17 :	
18 :	
19 :	
20 :	
21 :	

NOTES

#AlhamdulillahFor Everything

For the fourth week
of gratitude,
think about the things you feel
really strong about,
but you couldn't fit them
in previous categories.
Anything that you'd like to
thank and praise Allah for.
Do this each day for the next 10 days
until you finish all the given spaces
from day 22 to day 31.
There is a "notes" section at the end
of your list so you can write down
what you felt after one month of
your 'Alhamdulillah' journey.

Alhamdulillah for

New beginnings

Alhamdulillah for

1001+ Muslim inventions

Alhamdulillah for

endless means of transportation

Alhamdulillah for

cool shades on hot days

Alhamdulillah for

toothpaste and toothbrush in one

Alhamdulillah for

wounds that made me strong

Alhamdulillah for

the unique sound of each letter

Day #	Alhamdulillah for . . .
22 :	
23 :	
24 :	
25 :	
26 :	
27 :	
28 :	

29 :

30 :

31 :

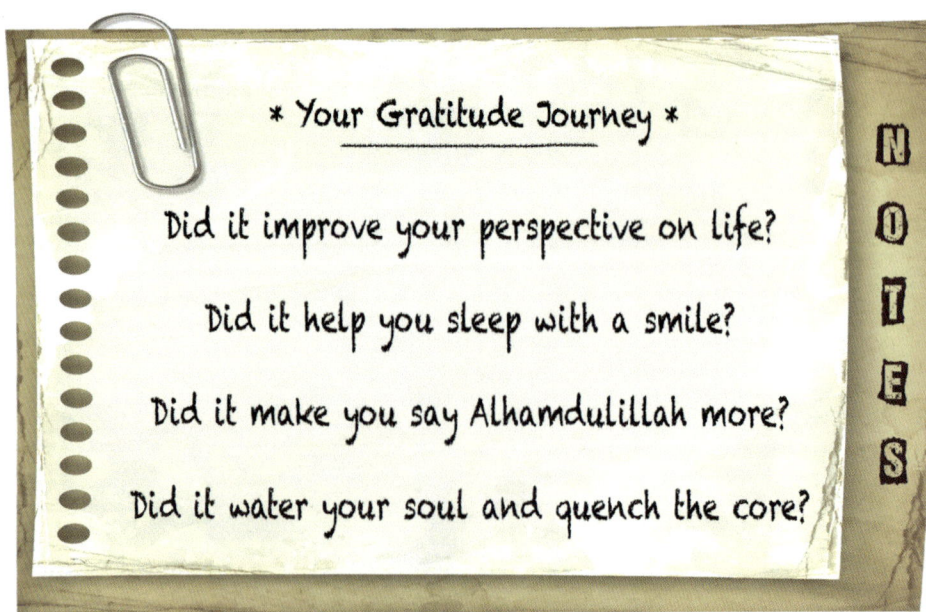

* Your Gratitude Journey *

Did it improve your perspective on life?

Did it help you sleep with a smile?

Did it make you say Alhamdulillah more?

Did it water your soul and quench the core?

NOTES

Alhamdulillah for

YOUR support

جزاك الله خيرا

"Whoever is not grateful to the people, he is not grateful to Allah."

[Jami` at-Tirmidhi]

[Book 27, Hadith 60]

Submit your art or ideas (or both) for #AlhamdulillahForSeries

Email: submissions @ ayeina.com

facebook.com/ayeina.online

@ayeina_official

Printed in Great Britain
by Amazon